A Child's First Library of Learning

Flowers and Trees

TIME-LIFE BOOKS • ALEXANDRIA, VIRGINIA

Contents

Why Do Plants Die Without Water?

ANSWER People need food and water to be strong and healthy. Plants do too. Green plants use water to make their own food. If they don't get enough water they will wilt and die.

If you water it...

▲ A wilted plant

◀ The plant will get much better.

Just How Do Flowers and Trees Get Water?

Flowers and trees draw water up through their roots. Each thick root has many thin roots to catch water.

Look at how many roots there are for just this one sunflower plant.

● **To the Parent**

All living things, including the human body, which is composed of more than 60% water, will perish without enough water. Plants use light, carbon dioxide and water to manufacture their own nutrients, a process called photosynthesis. The tree absorbs the water through a root system made up of thousands of very fine root hairs that increase the total area of the system and thus allow the plant to absorb more water.

TRY THIS

If you water only the flowers and leaves of a plant it will soon begin to wilt. Since plants and trees get water from their roots, you must sprinkle the water on the soil. The roots will draw the water from the soil up into the plant and it will grow strong and beautiful.

5

Do Plants Sleep at Night?

ANSWER Some plants close up at night, but this does not mean that the plant is asleep. If you make it as bright and warm as daytime, these plants will stay open just as they do during the day.

■ **Daytime**

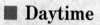

■ **Nighttime**

● **To the Parent**

Sleep is essential to higher animals, since the brain must rest. Human babies need 18 to 20 hours of sleep a day. An adult needs from 7 to 9 hours. Humans would probably die of exhaustion if they had to stay awake for days at a time. But plants have no brain and do not require sleep like people do. Rather, the closing of the plant leaves and flowers as shown here are reflex actions to darkness or drops in temperature.

❓ Do Plants Breathe?

ANSWER Yes, they do. Their leaves and stems have tiny holes that are too small to see. These holes are called stomata. Flowers and trees breathe in and out through these holes. They breathe a little differently at night than they do during the day, as you can see in the pictures below.

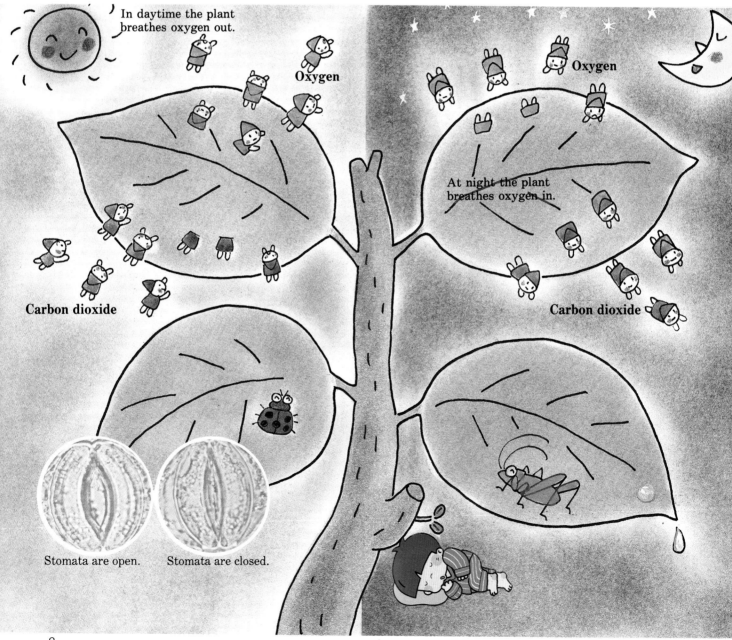

In daytime the plant breathes oxygen out.

Oxygen

Oxygen

At night the plant breathes oxygen in.

Carbon dioxide

Carbon dioxide

Stomata are open.

Stomata are closed.

▲ **The trunk of a large cedar.** It takes in air through the many cracks in its bark.

The oxygen we breathe is made by plants

The air is made of different gases. Oxygen is one of these. It is very important to people. We breathe in air, because we need oxygen to live. Green plants make oxygen. During the daytime, they send it into the air all around us. If all the flowers and trees in the world were to dry up and die, there would be no oxygen to breathe. That is why flowers and trees are so important to people and all other animals. If there were no trees and flowers, we would not be able to live on our planet.

● **To the Parent**

All living things, including plants, breathe. During the day, plants breathe in carbon dioxide. The combination of this gas with water and the energy of sunlight allows plants to manufacture their own nutrients by a process that is called photosynthesis. Oxygen is released as a result of this process. At other times, the plants breathe in oxygen and release carbon dioxide the way humans do. These gases pass not only through the stomata found in a plant's leaves, but also through pores in the branches and trunks of trees.

What Are Pistils and Stamens?

(ANSWER) Pistils and stamens are very important parts of a flower. Most flowers have a pistil in the center and several stamens around it. The pistil has a sticky top. The tip of each stamen is covered with a powder called pollen. When some of the pollen gets on the sticky pistil the plant is able to make fruit. The fruit has seeds inside, and new plants grow from those.

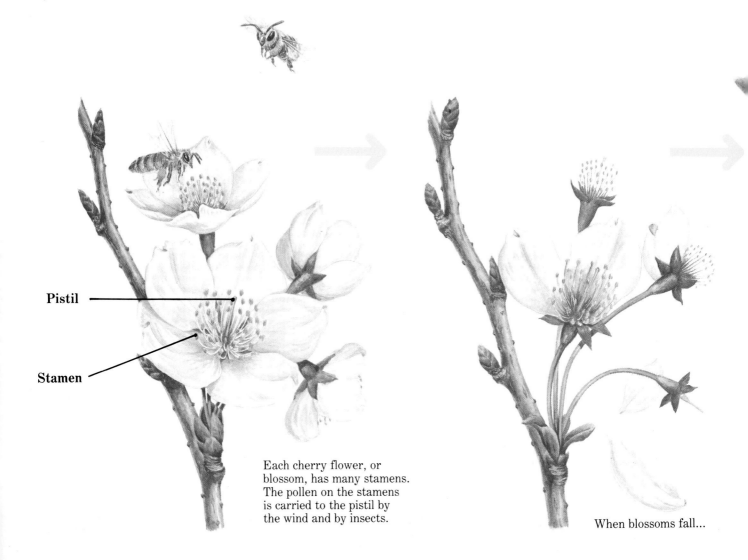

Pistil

Stamen

Each cherry flower, or blossom, has many stamens. The pollen on the stamens is carried to the pistil by the wind and by insects.

When blossoms fall...

Male and Female Flowers

Most flowers have a pistil and stamens. But some plants have two types of flowers: a female one, which has only a pistil, and a male, with stamens only.

▲ This female flower has only a pistil.

Cherries grow.

▲ This male flower has only stamens.

11

Why Are Flowers Beautiful?

ANSWER Many flowers need insects to help them make seeds. That is why they are so pretty. Flowers have bright colors to attract insects. Flowers also have a sweet-smelling liquid called nectar. When insects come to drink this nectar their bodies get covered with pollen. When some of this pollen rubs off on the flower's pistil the flower can make seeds.

■ How insects see flower colors

Insects get a different picture of flowers than people do because they have very different eyes.

A human's view

A honeybee's view

● To the Parent

Pollen is carried to the pistil of flowers either by wind or by insects. Plants that are fertilized by the wind, such as rice, wheat and pine trees, have inconspicuous flowers as a rule. But plants that are fertilized by insects are usually very bright and filled with nectar to attract the insects. Yet insects see them quite differently than humans. Honeybees are very sensitive to ultraviolet light, as the photo shows.

How Do We Make Perfume From Flowers?

(ANSWER) Insects are not the only ones that like sweet-smelling flowers. People like them, too. That's why we make perfume. To make perfume, people pick flowers and remove the oil from them. The oil is mixed with other scents to make perfume.

Perfume is made from a flower's aromatic oil.

• To the Parent

People have been making perfume for thousands of years. It is made by extracting aromatic oil from flower blossoms either by steam distillation or with chemical solvents. The oil is blended with other natural and synthetic materials to make perfume. Most paper is made from wood pulp that has been boiled under pressure and chemically treated. Cinnamon is made from the ground bark of several species of laurel trees. Charcoal is wood that has been partly burned. It is used for cooking and other purposes. Natural rubber is produced from latex, a liquid extracted from rubber trees.

■ Things that we make from trees

Paper

Cinnamon

Charcoal

Rubber

❓ Why Do We Plant Tulips and Hyacinths in the Fall?

ANSWER If their bulbs don't spend the winter in the earth they will not bear pretty flowers in the spring. Tulip and hyacinth bulbs can stand very cold weather. They grow roots and buds while it is still winter. Then as soon as it becomes warm their flowers bloom. If you plant tulips and hyacinths in the spring they will not grow very well. These plants grow best in places where the weather changes from one season to the next.

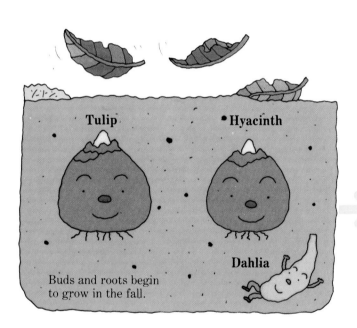

Tulip · Hyacinth

Dahlia

Buds and roots begin to grow in the fall.

They get longer during winter.

■ Bulbs that grow in the winter

Plant them in the fall, and they bloom in the spring.

These bulbs were planted in the fall.

Crocus

Anemone

Narcissus

● To the Parent

Usually flowers that bloom in early spring are resistant to cold and are planted in the fall. Flowers that bloom in the summer and fall are not very resistant to the cold and are planted in the spring. When bulbs that are not very resistant to the cold are planted in the fall they remain dormant during the winter and produce no bulbs or roots. Likewise, if cold-resistant bulbs are planted in spring, their flowers bloom late and damage easily in warm weather.

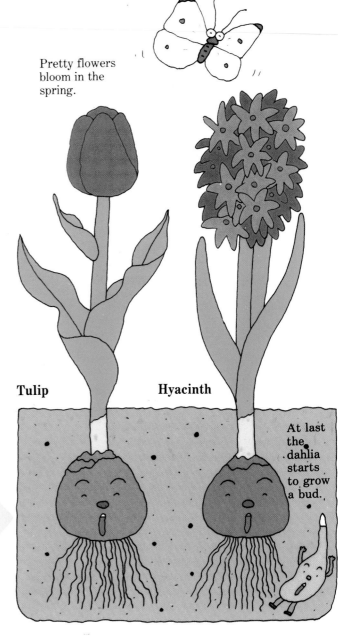

Pretty flowers bloom in the spring.

Tulip   **Hyacinth**

When it gets warm, up and up they grow.

At last the dahlia starts to grow a bud.

■ Bulbs that bloom in summer

Some bulbs like the dahlia don't grow in winter. They are planted in the spring, and their flowers bloom only in the summer.

Dahlia   **Gladiolus**   **Amaryllis**

17

Why Does the Wild Rose Have Thorns?

ANSWER The rose's thorns protect its leaves, flowers and buds from being eaten by wild animals and birds. The sharp thorns are very painful if you touch them. There are many other plants that have thorns to protect them from their enemies.

Other Plants With Thorns

▲ **Thistle.** It has thorns around its leaves.

▲ **Orange.** The tree branches have thorns.

▲ **Cactus.** It grows thorns instead of leaves.

● To the Parent

Plants have many different types of thorns. Some of them are located on the plant's stalk, as is the case of the wild rose bramble. In others the thorns might grow on the branches as on the orange tree, or they may grow instead of leaves as they do on the cactus. Some thorns contain poison. All of them, though, are for the plant's self-defense.

❓ Why Do Sunflowers Turn to Face the Sun?

Morning

ANSWER When the sunflower is young and is growing fast it turns toward the sun as it grows. The reason for that is that the part of the sunflower's stalk that is on the side away from the sun always grows faster than the stalk on the side facing the sun.

■ How sunflower stalks grow

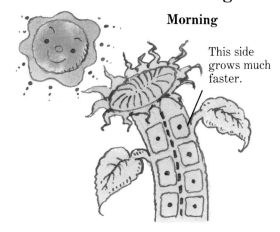

Morning

This side grows much faster.

Noon

Both sides grow at the same rate.

Evening

This side grows faster.

Afternoon

In the morning young sunflowers turn to the east. During the day they follow the sun. In the afternoon they lean to the west.

■ A fully grown sunflower

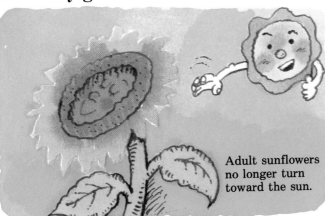

Adult sunflowers no longer turn toward the sun.

Why Do Blossoms Fall?

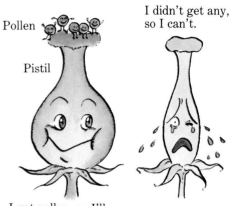

Pollen

I didn't get any, so I can't.

Pistil

ANSWER Blossoms fall to make room for a flower's fruit. A flower's pistil swells after it traps some pollen. After the blossoms fall the fruit, which is filled with seeds, starts to grow from the pistil. When the seeds fall to the ground new plants will grow from them. Later, the plants will grow new blossoms of their own.

I got pollen, so I'll be able to grow fruit.

▲ Pansy

▲ Eggplant

Ripe seeds inside opened pods.

The seeds are inside the fruit.

Flowers with many petals often do not have pistils and stamens, so they are not able to grow fruit.

▲ **Double-flowered peony**

If tulips grow fruit, their bulbs will not become large. That is why tulips are cut when they are almost finished blooming.

▲ **Sunflower**

▲ **Tulip**

It has many, many seeds.

It grows from a bulb.

❓ Why Do Trees Grow So Big?

(ANSWER) Flowers and trees grow during the spring and summer. In the fall and winter, flowers dry up, but the trees continue to grow slowly. Trees usually live longer than people. But unlike people, who stop growing when they become adults, trees grow as long as they live. That is why they grow so large.

Trees usually live longer than people.

Summer

Trees and flowers grow fast.

Fall

Flowers dry up and tree leaves fall.

Trees keep getting bigger as long as they live.

● To the Parent

Tree growth occurs at the same time above and below ground. Some redwood trees in the United States are more than 330 feet (100m) in height and 33 feet (10m) in diameter. Although redwoods originally sprouted from a single seed, these trees have gradually grown to giant size over a period of several thousand years.

Spring

Winter

The flowers have dried up and left only a bulb or seed. But trees stay throughout the winter.

Flowers sprout and trees bud, and begin to grow again. Trees grow stronger and taller than before.

25

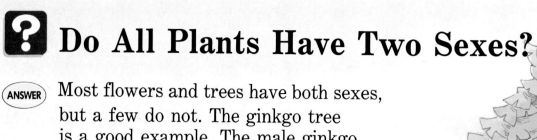 Do All Plants Have Two Sexes?

ANSWER Most flowers and trees have both sexes, but a few do not. The ginkgo tree is a good example. The male ginkgo tree has only stamens. They are covered with pollen. The female has only pistils. When the pollen from the male tree reaches the pistils of the female, the female tree starts producing ginkgo nuts.

A female ginkgo tree

■ Plants that have male and female types
The plants that grow the fruit are always the females.

▲ Female fern flowers have pistils for fruit.

▲ Male fern flowers have stamens but no pistils.

▲ Female pussy willow flowers with pistils.

▲ Male pussy willow flowers with stamens.

▲ Female tree
with pistils

▲ Male tree
with stamens

A male ginkgo tree

▲ Female laurel flowers
with pistils for fruit.

▲ Male laurel flowers
with stamens only.

● **To the Parent**

Unlike most animals where the sexes are separate, most plants are hermaphroditic: they have both male and female reproductive organs. Among plants it is not very hard to count the ones in which the male and female are separate. They include the ginkgo tree, hemp plant, laurel, fern and mulberry. Ginkgo nuts are produced by the female tree, but this requires that the pollen from flowers of the male tree be deposited on the pistils of the female. Otherwise the tree will not produce nuts.

❓ Did You Know that Some Plants Live Off Other Plants?

ANSWER The mistletoe, for one, sends roots into certain trees. It grows by taking water and food from the tree it has joined. It also makes its own food, but never enough. That's why if the tree that the mistletoe is joined to dies, the mistletoe also dies. In many parts of the world mistletoe is a Christmas decoration.

▲ Mistletoe growing on an oak tree

Cut a tree where the mistletoe has joined itself, and you can see wedge-shaped roots growing into it.

● **To the Parent**

Plants that attach themselves to other plants or trees and take nutrients from them are called parasites. Among them are those like the mistletoe, which have green leaves and produce some nutrients themselves, and those like the broomrape and dodder, which make nothing themselves. All die when the host tree dies. The dodder sends out many tendrils in search of new hosts. It can greatly damage other plant life.

Some More Plants that Live Off Others

▲ **A medical parasite.** This grows by taking water and food from the roots of the scrub oak.

▲ **Broomrape.** It gets its water and food from the roots of the eulalia.

▲ **Dodder.** It grows by winding itself around many types of plants and taking their food.

29

Why Do Leaves Change Color When It Gets Cold?

ANSWER Leaves contain a lot of green material called chlorophyll. They also have a yellow substance called carotene, which gives carrots their color. When weather becomes cold, chlorophyll breaks down, so we can see the yellow. When it gets cold the food in leaves also turns red, which is why some leaves turn red. Trees remain green if the chlorophyll in their leaves does not break down, even in very cold weather. These are called evergreen trees.

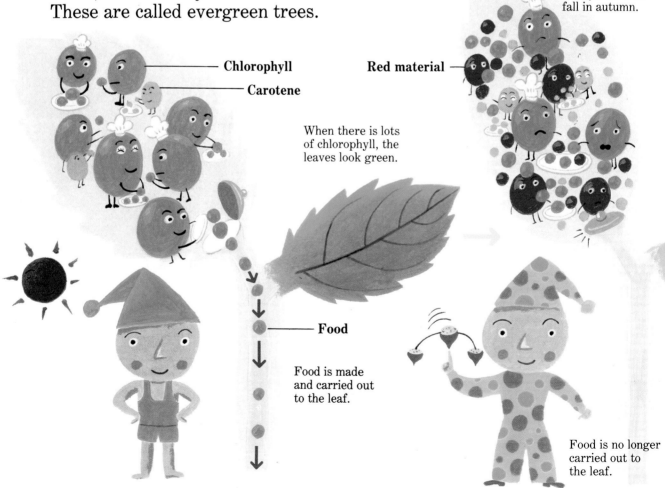

The green leaves turn yellow and fall in autumn.

Chlorophyll

Carotene

Red material

When there is lots of chlorophyll, the leaves look green.

Food

Food is made and carried out to the leaf.

Food is no longer carried out to the leaf.

Spring and summer

Fall

■ Leaves that turn red or yellow when it gets cold

▲ **Maple.** The leaves make red material and carotene too, so they turn bright red.

▲ **Ginkgo.** Its leaves have only carotene after the chlorophyll goes away, so they turn yellow.

The leftover food has turned red, so the leaves are red.

After a while leaves that have changed color will fall off the tree. These dead leaves will rot and fertilize the soil.

Winter

● **To the Parent**

Leaves are a green color because they contain a large amount of chlorophyll. They also contain a yellow and orange substance called carotene. In colder climates the chlorophyll breaks down in fall, and the carotene makes the leaves appear yellow or orange. Further, the nutrients, or anthocyanins, in the leaves turn red when temperatures drop and it gets chilly. Differing amounts of these substances create a variety of autumn colors. These changes are not very common in tropical climates.

Why Do Some Trees Lose Their Leaves in Winter?

ANSWER During winter in the northern countries there are fewer hours of light each day than in spring or summer. It is colder, too. This means that the roots and leaves of certain kinds of trees take a rest. The trees do this by dropping their leaves until spring comes again.

▲ **A cherry tree in winter**

■ Getting ready for the coming of spring

Even though its leaves have fallen, a tree doesn't rest completely. It is busy making buds that will form new leaves and flowers in spring.

Stamens

Pistil

A flower bud

A leaf bud with a tiny leaf just beginning.

▲ **A cherry tree buds during winter**

The beginnings of the pistil and stamens are inside the bud, as you see here.

■ Some trees keep their leaves in winter

There are some trees that can stand the cold better than others. Pine trees are among those that do not mind the cold and do not lose their leaves even in winter. When spring comes and their new leaves come out, the older leaves just drop off. We call these trees evergreens.

Spring

Winter

▲ **Cedar trees.** They keep their leaves in the winter.

■ Trees that flower in winter

Camellia

Sasanqua

Why Do Tree Trunks Have So Many Rings?

(ANSWER) Like flowers and grasses, trees do not die in winter. They continue to grow. When you look at a tree trunk that has been cut, you see many rings. The lighter rings are where the tree grew quickly in the warm days of spring and summer. The darker rings are where the tree grew more slowly in the cool of fall. Trees that have been living for a long time have many rings.

▲ One ring is made each year, so by counting the rings of the trunk you can find out how old the tree was when it was cut down.

Spring and Summer

The tree grows quickly, making the light rings.

Fall

It grows slower now, making dark rings.

▲ Winter is for sleep.

The next fall

It grows a little more and adds a dark ring.

The next spring and summer

Now it grows very fast and adds another light ring.

34

The oldest living thing

Some trees have been alive for thousands of years. Bristlecone pines are believed to be the oldest trees in the world. Some of them are almost 5,000 years old.

● **To the Parent**

Beneath its bark is a tree's cambium layer, where new cell tissue is added to the trunk. A tree trunk's rings grow year by year. By counting the growth rings of a tree you can determine its age. Most authorities believe that the bristlecone pines in the western part of the United States are the oldest living trees. Other very old trees are the Jomon cedar on the Japanese island of Yakushima and the Montezuma cypress at Oaxaca, Mexico.

❓ How Big Do Trees Grow?

ANSWER Trees come in many sizes. The biggest trees in the world are the giant redwood trees that grow in northern California. Some of them are as tall as 385 feet (117 m).

It's as high as a 14-story building. That's tall!

■ Some other interesting trees

The coco-de-mer palm has the largest seed.

The tropical banyan tree has the most trunks.

The Jomon cedar is one of the widest trees.

Dwarf trees are the world's smallest trees.

● To the Parent

The giant redwood, which is found along the west coast of the United States, is the world's tallest tree, while the sequoias are the biggest in bulk. At the other extreme, dwarf trees are the smallest. They grow naturally in the harsh weather of the Arctic. One seed of the coco-de-mer palm can weigh as much as 50 pounds (22 kg). The many trunks of a banyan tree are actually thick aerial roots that have developed from the tree's branches and dropped to take root in the soil. The trunk of the Jomon cedar measures 140 feet (43 m) in circumference at ground level.

? Why Do Seeds Stick to Us?

ANSWER Seeds need to travel to new places so they can spread and grow. Since seeds cannot travel by themselves, they sometimes stick to our clothes and to the fur of animals. In this way they are carried from their parent plant to a place where they can grow and make their own seeds.

■ Sticky seeds

These stick with burrs

◀ This has only two needles, but it sticks as though it had twenty.

◀ You can't see the burrs, but you will know when this one sticks to you.

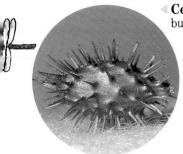

◀ **Cocklebur.** It has many burrs to help it stick.

And these are just sticky

◀ Eight nodules might mean that it is eight times as sticky!

◀ It's pretty, all right, and it's sticky, too.

39

How Do Acorns Become Oak Trees?

ANSWER Oak trees drop many acorns in the fall. Almost all of them rot or are eaten by field mice. But some acorns start to grow a root during the winter, and when the spring comes a leaf appears. As it becomes warmer and the sun shines on them, they grow bigger.

Winter

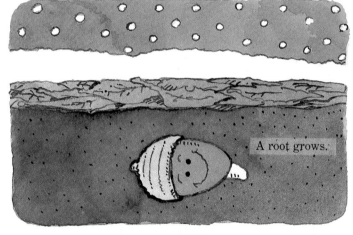

A root grows.

▲ A root, or sprout, coming out the end of an acorn.

It takes about ten years for an acorn to grow up and become a sturdy tree.

Spring

Leaves grow.

▲ In time the sprout turns into a leaf.

▲ Then it grows more leaves to become a young tree.

41

Why Are Chestnut Burrs So Thorny?

ANSWER The chestnut is the seed of the chestnut tree. This seed is very important if a new chestnut tree is to grow. To protect it from being eaten by animals, the chestnut has sharp thorns on its cover, or burr. When the seed is ready to grow, the burr bursts open and the seed pops out.

And How Else Are Tree Seeds Protected?

Many trees grow seeds inside their fruit. If the seeds are not ready to grow, the fruit tastes sour or bitter. People and animals do not like it. When the seeds are ready the fruit has a sweet taste.

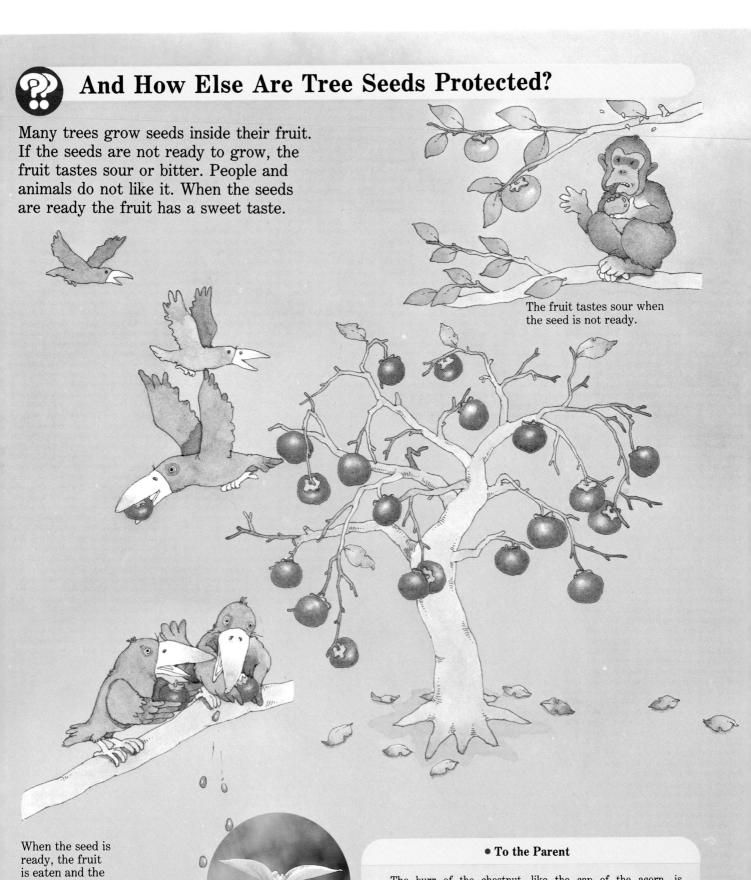

The fruit tastes sour when the seed is not ready.

When the seed is ready, the fruit is eaten and the seeds are dropped.

A new sprout

● To the Parent

The burr of the chestnut, like the cap of the acorn, is a modification of that portion of the pistillate flower known as the protective sheath. The thorns on the chestnut burr are a self-defense mechanism. An immense number of tree seeds are surrounded by the flesh of the fruit, which will not be edible until the seed is ready to germinate.

? Why Are Dandelions So Fluffy?

ANSWER The flower of the dandelion is really a large number of small flowers bunched together. After dandelions bloom, each of their many flowers makes a seed. Each seed has white, fluffy threads attached to it by a long stem. The wind blows this fluff away, and the seed is carried with it. When the seed comes down to the ground again it will sprout and grow into a new dandelion. So when you blow the fluff away you may be helping another dandelion grow.

The seed floats to the ground.

It puts down roots.

Soon a new dandelion grows.

⚙ Why Are Some Bananas Without Seeds?

ANSWER All bananas had seeds at one time. But the seeds made them hard to eat. So the people who grew the kind of bananas that we like to eat found a way to grow them without big seeds.

▲ At one time, all bananas had large seeds like the ones you see in this photograph.

The bananas that we usually eat have been grown without the seeds.

If bananas had big seeds they would be hard to eat.

How Are New Bananas Grown Without Seeds?

New sprouts grow from the roots of the banana tree. These are cut off and replanted, and new trees with seedless bananas grow from them. Bananas grow only in the warm tropical countries.

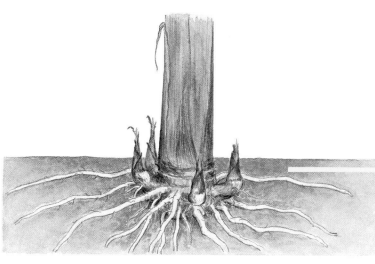

The sprouts are cut off and planted.

Other kinds of tasty fruit without seeds

All the fruits here usually have seeds. But scientists have found ways to grow these delicacies without seeds.

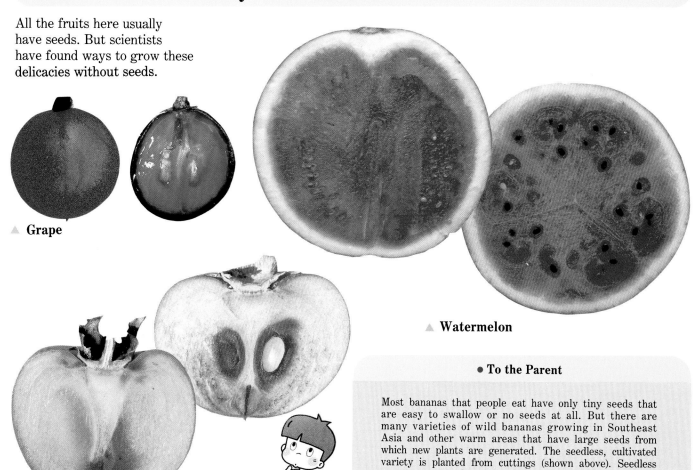

▲ Grape

▲ Watermelon

▲ Persimmon

● To the Parent

Most bananas that people eat have only tiny seeds that are easy to swallow or no seeds at all. But there are many varieties of wild bananas growing in Southeast Asia and other warm areas that have large seeds from which new plants are generated. The seedless, cultivated variety is planted from cuttings (shown above). Seedless grapes are produced by dipping their flowers into a chemical. In a similar manner watermelons are rendered seedless by chemical treatment.

How Can a Fig Tree Make Fruit When It Has No Flowers?

The flower blooms inside the fruit.

ANSWER Oh, but fig trees **do** have flowers. We can't see them because they bloom right inside the figs. The flowers inside these figs have pistils and stamens like other flowers, and they also make seeds. In fact when you eat a fig and feel something gritty inside your mouth you are eating the seeds. Fig trees live the longest of all fruit trees, sometimes as long as 2,000 years. Ordinarily they bear two crops of fruit each year.

The place where all these small flowers are is called the torus. It becomes a fig.

Torus

The flower of the fig tree is inside here.

When the torus is fully grown, it becomes sweet.

Pistil

Stamen

Which Ones Are Flowers?

Here we see what looks like some very pretty flowers. But many of them are not really flowers at all. Flowers have many secrets for us to learn.

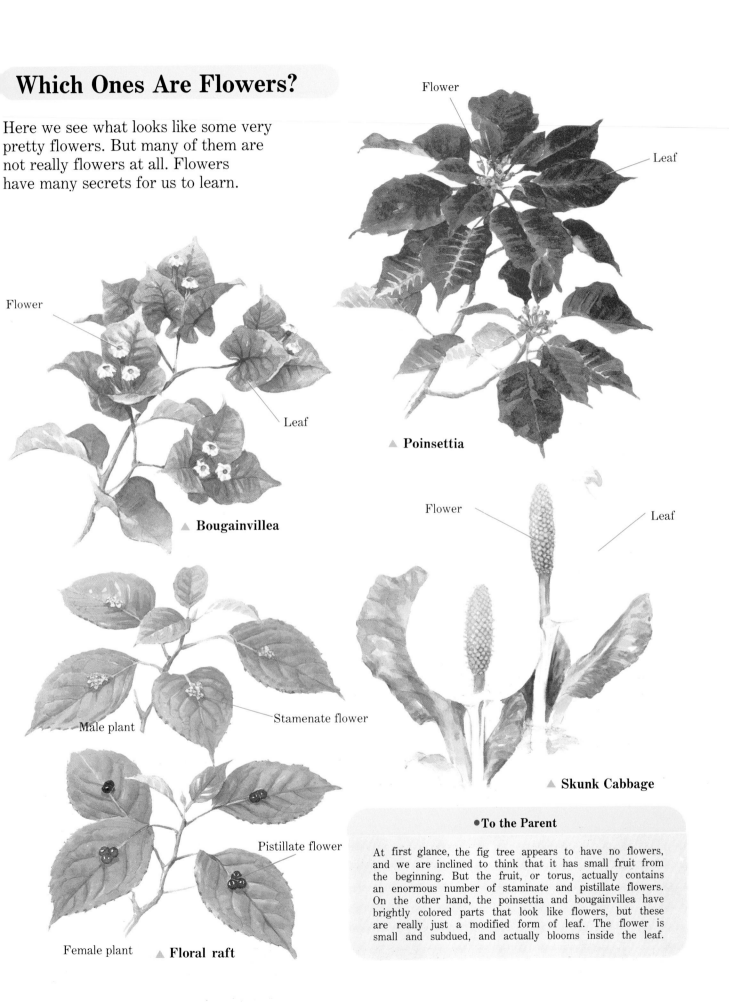

Flower

Leaf

▲ **Poinsettia**

Flower

Leaf

Male plant

Stamenate flower

▲ **Skunk Cabbage**

Flower

Leaf

▲ **Bougainvillea**

Pistillate flower

Female plant   ▲ **Floral raft**

●To the Parent

At first glance, the fig tree appears to have no flowers, and we are inclined to think that it has small fruit from the beginning. But the fruit, or torus, actually contains an enormous number of staminate and pistillate flowers. On the other hand, the poinsettia and bougainvillea have brightly colored parts that look like flowers, but these are really just a modified form of leaf. The flower is small and subdued, and actually blooms inside the leaf.

How Does Wild Grass Grow Without Any Plant Food?

(ANSWER) Fields and hillsides in the wild are covered with dead flowers and plants. As they rot, food found inside them goes into the soil to become fertilizer. The grass uses this food to grow. On farmland the crops are cut and the food does not return to the soil, so farmers add fertilizer.

▲ Horsetails sprout from among dead grasses.

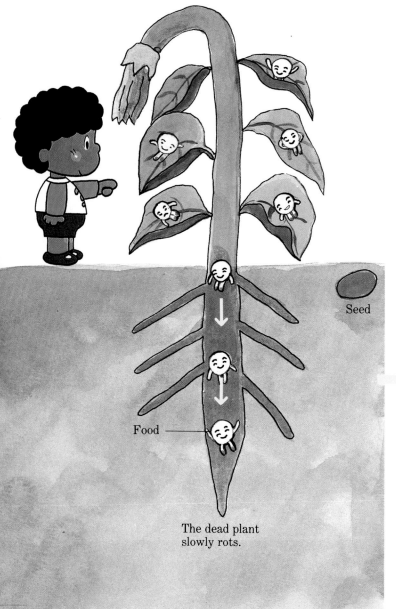

Seed

Food

The dead plant slowly rots.

Its food enters the soil as fertilizer.

Ashes from burning dead grass make fertilizer.

● **To the Parent**

Plants create a certain amount of their own nutrient needs through the process of photosynthesis. The rest of it is picked up from the soil by the plant's roots. The plant's most essential nutrients are nitrogen, phosphorus and potassium, which are the three principal constituents of fertilizer. In the wild, withered grass, fallen leaves and the bodies of small animals decompose to form a natural fertilizer. Worm and mite feces constitute another.

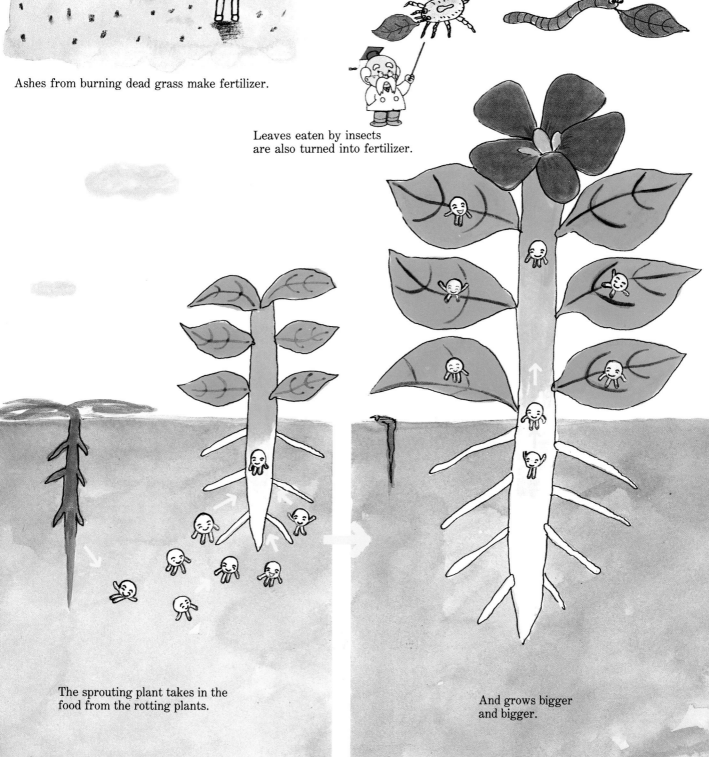

Leaves eaten by insects
are also turned into fertilizer.

The sprouting plant takes in the
food from the rotting plants.

And grows bigger
and bigger.

Why Do We Dig Up the Earth Before We Plant Seeds?

ANSWER We dig up the earth before planting to make it easier for the seeds to sprout. This helps air mix into the soil and lets water soak in better. Digging up the soil causes insects to run away or die, and kills weeds. We also remove rocks and stones when we dig up the soil. All this helps the seeds grow better.

■ **If we dig up the earth...**

Air

Air

Our digging helped make the plants healthier.

In soil that has been carefully dug, plant
roots quickly grow downward and sideways.

■ If we don't dig up the earth...

They don't look so healthy.
I wonder what's wrong?

53

❓ Why Do We Pull Weeds?

(ANSWER) Weeds are very strong and take away the water and fertilizer we use to help vegetables and other foods grow better. If this happens, the vegetables will not be able to grow big. Also, if the weeds grow tall, the vegetables will not get as much sunshine as they need. By pulling the weeds out, we make sure the vegetables get all the water, fertilizer and sunshine that they need to become big.

▲ When left alone, weeds grow very fast.

If we don't pull the weeds out...

They will harm the vegetables.

■ Weeds are very strong

They use up food and water.

Stomping doesn't hurt them.

If the roots are left, they grow again.

How Do Weeds Grow When Nobody Plants Their Seeds?

The wind helps weeds grow in fields by blowing large numbers of the weeds' seeds to other places. When the seeds fall they soon start to grow.

Winds carry the seeds.

Some roots grow sideways and sprout many times.

■ Some weeds have pretty flowers

▲ Many kinds of weeds grow fast in rice fields.

▲ Daisy fleabane grows when grass is left uncut.

▲ The henbit likes to grow in sunny places.

❓ Does a Cactus Have Leaves?

ANSWER Yes. The sharp spines on the cactus are its leaves. The cactus can grow in very dry places like deserts. To keep it from losing its water, the cactus leaves are very small. These leaves have very sharp thorns to protect the cactus plant from birds and animals that would otherwise eat it.

Prickly pear

Saguaro

■ Cactus plants store water

In deserts, there are long periods of time when no rain falls. This is why the cactus has roots that can quickly pick up even the smallest amounts of water. It stores this water in its stem. When there is no rain for a long time it uses this water little by little.

When no rain falls, the cactus uses the water in its stem, and the stem gets thinner and thinner.

▲ A stem grown thin by using up its water

▼ **Spines of a cactus**

Pincushion cactus

Barrel cactus

Barrel cactus

Hedgehog cactus

● **To the Parent**

The parts of the cactus that at first sight look like leaves are really stems. The leaves have been changed into spines. This adaptation is very convenient for desert plants that must withstand long periods without rainfall. The cactus and other plants that can store water are a valuable source of food and drink for thirsty desert animals. On the other hand the cactus spines are useful in protecting it from these animals.

The cactus has many roots. They do not go deep into the soil, so that they can quickly collect water near the surface when it rains.

▲ **The stem of a cactus that has taken in a lot of rain water**

❓ Why Is Bamboo Hollow?

ANSWER The bamboo plant grows from shoots. If you cut a bamboo shoot down the middle you can see that the joints are close together. As the shoot grows it doesn't become any wider, but the distance between the joints gets longer. As it lengthens, long, hollow chambers form inside the bamboo plant.

▲ **A bamboo grove.** New shoots are everywhere.

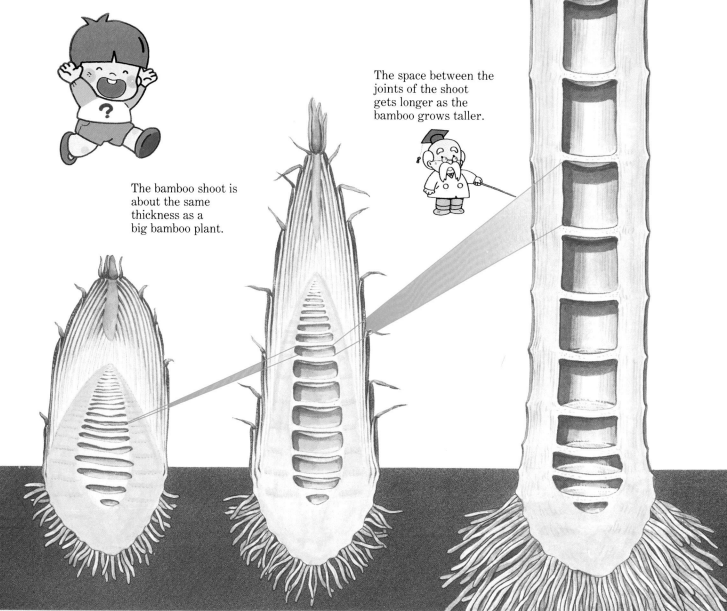

The bamboo shoot is about the same thickness as a big bamboo plant.

The space between the joints of the shoot gets longer as the bamboo grows taller.

The Bamboo's Secret

Bamboo shoots are new growths that sprout from stalks that run under the ground. These shoots develop very fast. Some kinds can grow as tall as you are in a single day. Bamboo plants also have flowers. Soon after the flowers blossom the bamboo plant dies.

Bamboo shoots grow from stalks that run underground.

▲ A close-up view of bamboo flowers

Some shoots that were this high yesterday...

Will be as tall as you are today!

● **To the Parent**

Bamboo is not really a tree, but in fact is a member of the grass family. Trees have a formative layer called cambium that enables them to grow thicker with time, but grasses do not have this layer. So when bamboo has grown to a certain width it stops growing sideways and grows only vertically. Bamboo normally reproduces by sending up new shoots from an underground runner, but it also reproduces by the flowering process which produces seeds.

? What Is Corn Silk?

ANSWER Male flowers that have only stamens bloom at the top of the cornstalk. Female flowers with only pistils bloom beneath the husks. Many female flowers are grouped together. Each one has a long silken pistil. We call these pistils corn silk.

Can you guess who I am when I have my new corn-silk moustache on?

Male flowers

Female flowers

▲ **The pistils.** Each long pistil
is attached to one kernel of corn.

Female flowers have
long pistils that
look like silk.

Male flower pollen
blown by the wind
sticks to the pistils.

Ears of corn begin
to form. Kernels of
corn are seeds that
form below pistils.

❓ Why Does the Lotus Root Have Holes?

(ANSWER) There is very little air in the mud beneath lakes and ponds. Water plants like the lotus root and water lily need air to live. But they cannot get it from the mud, so their roots must breathe in another way. Air enters through the leaves, which float on top of the water. It travels through holes in the stem to the holes in the roots.

▲ **Lotus root**   ▲ **Leaf stem**

Mangrove trees grow along tropical coasts, where the mud flats they stand on are often flooded by the tide. Their roots stand above the top of the water so they can breathe.

● **To the Parent**

Although we apply the term lotus root to it, this part of the lotus plant is not, properly speaking, a root at all but part of the stem, or stalk. In adapting part of its stem to store food underground the lotus plant is, in a manner of speaking, similar to the potato. Since there is very little air in the mud underwater, plants with underwater roots must obtain their air in other ways.

? What Is a Horsetail?

ANSWER It is really two plants in one. During the winter it looks like the plants in the picture at the right. But in spring another type of plant sprouts from the same root and grows into the green plants shown below the horsetails. When one of these plants dies, the other comes up and replaces it.

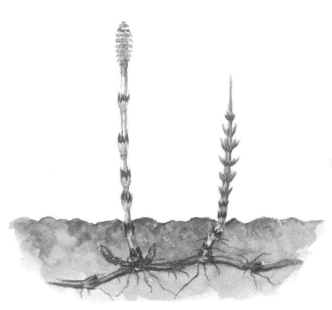

Reminds me of a paint brush.

In spring, a different-looking plant grows.

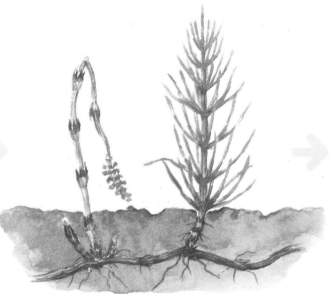

The winter horsetail withers and dies.

▲ When the snow melts, winter horsetails cover the ground. Horsetails grow in swampy, wet places all over the world.

▲ **Springtime.** The winter horsetails give way to new plants.

65

❓ Does the Cabbage Have Flowers?

ANSWER Yes, but usually the cabbages are picked before the flowers can bloom. At first the leaves of the cabbage are spread open. As it grows, they curl up to form a round head. If they aren't picked, the leaves open again and their flowers grow.

The stalk grows from here.

▲ Pretty yellow cabbage flowers

▲ A young cabbage cut in half

Cabbage leaves are spread open when they start out.

The leaves curl up to form the head we usually see.

The leaves open again and
a stalk begins to grow.

A fully grown cabbage
plant with pretty flowers.

❓ How Do Mushrooms Grow?

ANSWER Mushrooms grow from very tiny seeds called spores. Spores are found on the underside of the mushroom head. As tiny as dust, these spores float onto fallen leaves or dead trees and take food from them. Soon, mushrooms spring forth from the spores.

My tree seed is so much bigger.

The flybane grows among pine needles and fallen birch leaves.

Pinecone mushrooms grow from pinecones.

The stinkhorn grows among fallen leaves.

The morel grows in forests and meadows.

In some places mushrooms grow from cicada bodies.

Pine-tree mushrooms take food from the roots of pine trees.

This tree mushroom likes dead trees.

The bracket fungus grows on tree stumps.

● To the Parent

Mushrooms are propagated by spores, which are released from the underside of the mushroom's cap. These float on the wind or are carried by insects until they come to rest on dead trees or fallen leaves. The spores then sprout to form an underground network of minute, threadlike filaments that is called a mycelium. The mushroom develops from this root-like fungal network.

How Does the Venus's-flytrap Eat Insects?

(ANSWER) When the Venus's-flytrap catches a fly it changes the fly's flesh into a kind of thick juice that it can eat. When the juice is used up the plant opens its leaves again. The parts of the fly's body that were not used up will soon be blown away and only the fly's shadow will be left.

When a fly walks on the leaf, it quickly closes.

The fly is trapped. The edges of the leaf form bars like a cage, and the fly cannot escape.

The parts of the fly that are not eaten will be blown away.

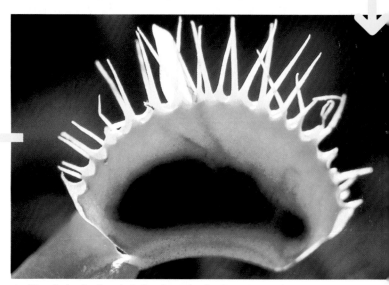

The fly's shadow is left when the leaf opens again.

■ Other plants that trap insects

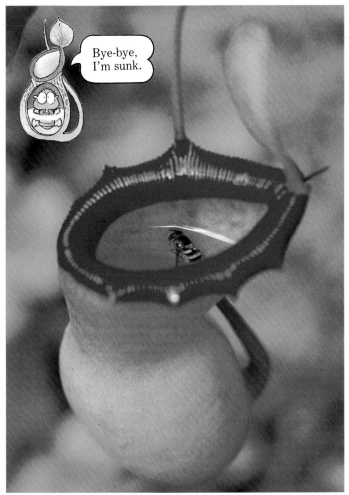

Bye-bye, I'm sunk.

▲ **Pitcher plant.** It lives off insects that fall into its pitcher, or bowl.

Oh no, I slipped.

▲ **Sarracenia plant.** Its leaf is shaped like a bag. Insects that fall into it cannot escape.

▲ **Sundew plant.** It puts out a sticky juice around its flowers and insects get caught in it.

I'm stuck...

● **To the Parent**

Plants that catch insects and live off their nutrients are called insectivorous plants. The Venus's-flytrap exists only in a small area along the east coast of North America. When it traps a fly or other insect, the plant excretes a digestive fluid that dissolves the protein in the insect's body into a liquid form that it can absorb. The entire process lasts about one week. Insectivorous plants do not depend entirely on insects for survival, but those that trap and eat insects grow larger and stronger than plants without such a diet.

Why Do So Few Plants Grow Along the Seashore?

ANSWER The seashore is covered with sand, which cannot store water. When the wind blows, the sand covers the plants. And when the waves and tides come in, the plants are washed out to sea. Salt water and salty air kill most plants. Even so, there are some plants that do grow along the seashore.

Water, give me water!

This sand is so heavy!

Help! I'm drowning!

Ugh, that's too salty!

Bindweed

Sea bells

Some Seashore Plants

Plants that grow along the seashore can stand saltwater and do not die even when they are buried in the sand. After being buried for a while their shoots poke through the sand, and new flowers appear. These plants often have long roots that grow away from the edge of the ocean, toward fresh water.

Even if covered, new shoots soon poke through the sand.

The plants are joined under the sand.

This long runner lets it live on seashores.

Long roots let this plant reach fresh water.

Its root is not only long, but thick.

● **To the Parent**

The seashore is not hospitable to most plants. Strong sunshine and continuous, salt-laden winds preclude all ordinary plants from growing. Among the more common plants that are usually found along seashores are those belonging to the convolvulus family pictured on the opposite page. Mangrove trees thrive along tropical coasts that are regularly inundated with water, and these hardy specimens can be found all over the world.

▲ **Mangrove trees.** They can grow even in saltwater.

How Do Some Plants Float in the Water?

ANSWER Plants that live on top of the water have floats so that they will not sink. They also have roots that act as weights so that they will not turn over when the wind blows.

Water hyacinth

Duckweed

74

■ Parts of a float

Water hyacinth and duckweed plants have lots of empty spaces throughout. Their spaces are filled with air. That makes the plants light enough to float in water.

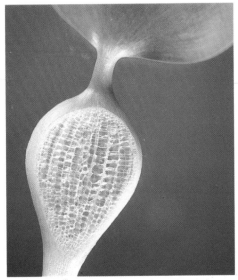

▲ A side view of the water hyacinth's float.

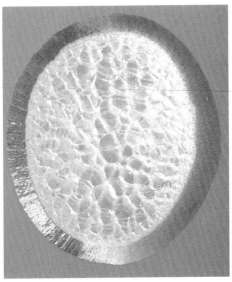

▲ Here we see the float's many spaces from the top.

■ The root acts as a balance

The roots of the water hyacinth and duckweed hang down in the water and act as weights so the plants do not tip over. The roots of these water plants also take in food from the water.

▲ Water hyacinth roots are bulky.

▲ Duckweed roots are very long.

■ Duckweed grows very fast

▲ If not pulled it can soon cover a paddy field.

● To the Parent

Plants adapt their forms to their environments. Water plants, which float and drift along with the currents and winds, have developed very differently from land plants. They have developed floats for buoyancy and root systems that serve as stabilizing weights. The water hyacinth can often be seen in goldfish tanks.

75

Why Do Flower Pots Have a Hole in the Bottom?

ANSWER The hole lets extra water run out. If too much water were to stay in the pot the roots would drown and the plant would die. For plants a little water fairly often is better than lots of water all at once.

Help! I'm drowning!

● To the Parent

If a flower pot is not properly drained, the water that collects in it can cause the roots and the plant itself to decay. Air cannot circulate freely unless it has both a way in and out. Without a hole in a pot, air circulation is poor and not enough air gets into the soil. The roots, which need air to breathe, will suffocate without enough of it. So the bottom hole is indispensable to flower pots. Also, pots should be porous so they can contribute to the "breathing" process.

Flower pots also have a hole in the bottom so that air can pass through freely. Without this hole there would not be enough air in the soil for the roots to stay healthy. When they get lots of air and just the right amount of water, plants grow extremely well.

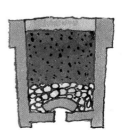

I need air.

Air

TRY THIS

If you keep these hints in mind when filling a flowerpot with soil, it will be easy for air and water to pass through the soil.

Place a small stone or a piece of pot over the hole.

Fill the bottom with gravel or a hard lump of soil.

Strain the soil through a sifter, then fill the pot.

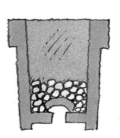

What Do We See Here?

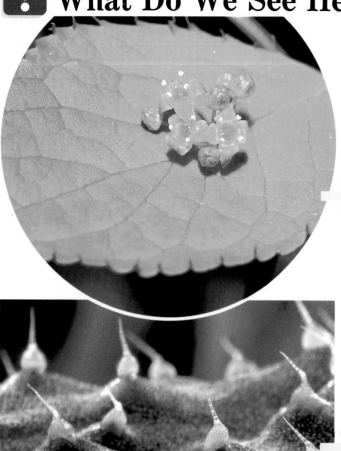

A leaf of the floral raft

In the spring a little green flower grows right in the center of this unusual plant.

Thorns on a cucumber

Small thorns can be seen on some types of cucumbers.

Banana-plant flowers

All these bananas come from just a single flower.

I don't think I can eat all of them.

■ Maple-tree seeds

They can fly through the air like a helicopter's propeller.

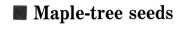

■ Pine-tree flowers

These female flowers will turn into pine cones.

■ Lotus-plant seeds

Each of the plant's seed pods has about 20 seeds inside. In this way just one lotus plant can make many more plants.

❓ And What Are These?

■ A morning glory

The hairy stems and leaves of the morning glory.

■ A straw insect guard

Insects on trees move into this straw cover to live through the winter. In spring the insects are killed when the straw is burned.

■ Snow supports for pine trees

These ropes are tied to the tree branches so that they will not break under the weight of the snow.

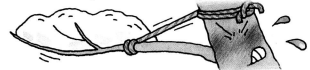

Growing-Up Album

Things I Made Myself

Kindergarten and elementary school children make many things from plants, flowers and fallen leaves, and this page is provided so their creations can be kept. These activities allow the child to become familiar with the shape and characteristics of various plants by hands-on experience. You may wish to take photographs of collages and other things made from plants, and paste them on this page.

Mount a photograph here

■ Flower-Dyeing and Collages

To do flower-dyeing, select various colored flower petals. Arrange them on a sheet of art paper, cover with another sheet, and pound them with a mallet. To make a collage, use glue to attach the petals to art paper, and photograph it before it fades.

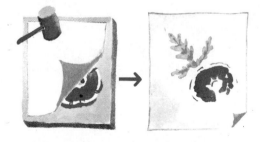

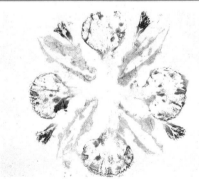

Mount the child's work here

■ Collage of Leaves

Collect fallen leaves of
various colors and glue
them to a sheet of art paper.
Then mark them with eyes,
arms, legs and other
characteristics to
create interesting designs.

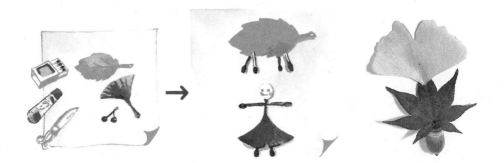

Mount the child's work here

■ Record of the child's questions about plants

Flower and Tree Riddles

Can you figure out what these different
plants are? Match each flower or tree in
the riddles with the ones in the pictures.

1. My branches are covered with thorns to protect
   my sweet-smelling flowers from my enemies.

2. During the day I turn my face to
   the sun as it moves across the sky.

3. I grow by putting my roots into other trees.
   I'm used as a decoration at Christmas time.

4. I grow from bulbs that are planted in the fall.

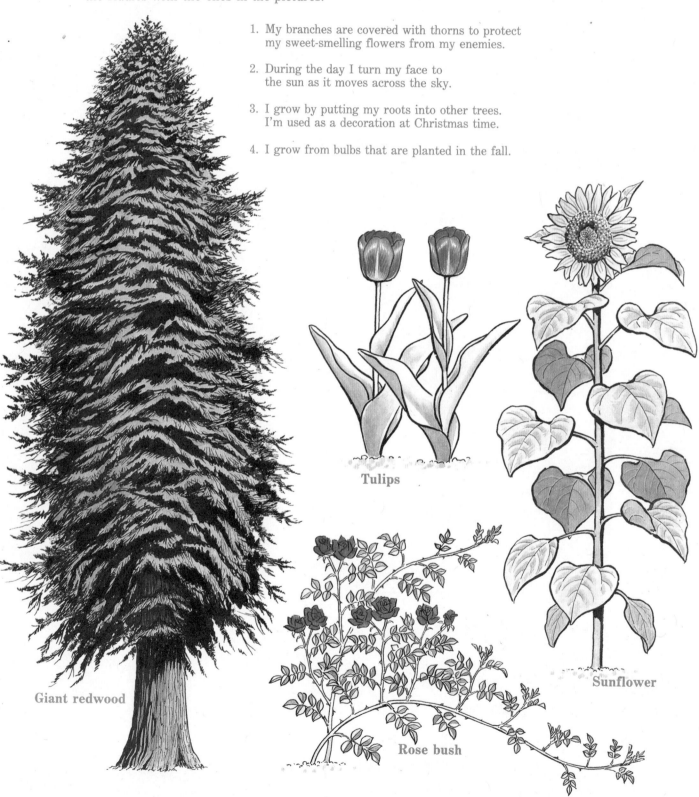

Giant redwood

Tulips

Sunflower

Rose bush

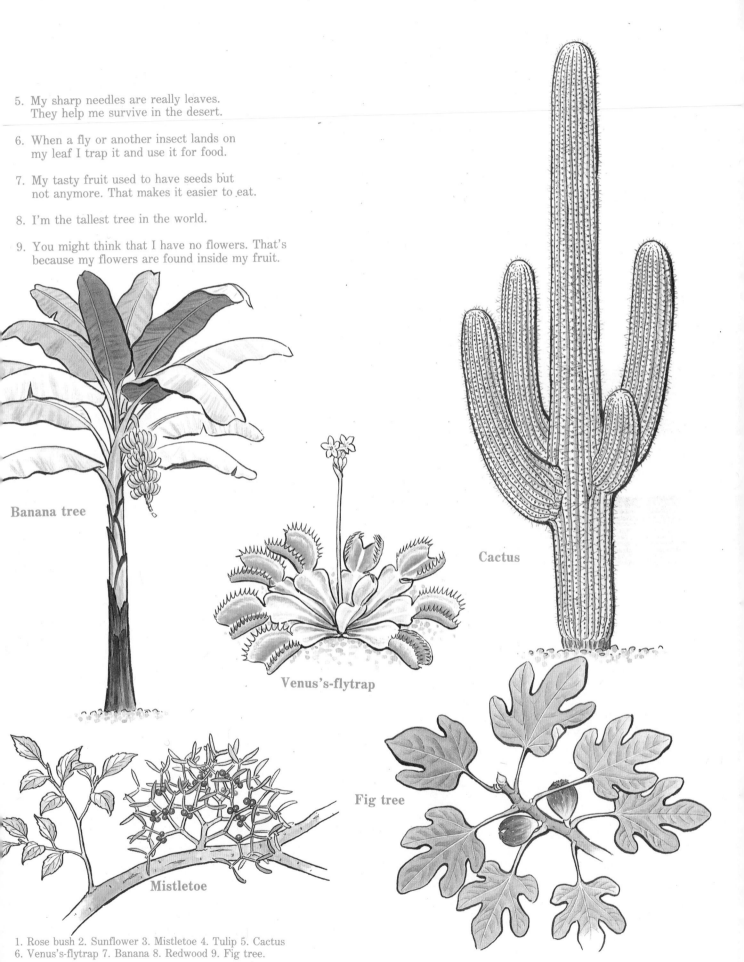

5. My sharp needles are really leaves.
   They help me survive in the desert.

6. When a fly or another insect lands on
   my leaf I trap it and use it for food.

7. My tasty fruit used to have seeds but
   not anymore. That makes it easier to eat.

8. I'm the tallest tree in the world.

9. You might think that I have no flowers. That's
   because my flowers are found inside my fruit.

Banana tree

Venus's-flytrap

Cactus

Mistletoe

Fig tree

1. Rose bush 2. Sunflower 3. Mistletoe 4. Tulip 5. Cactus
6. Venus's-flytrap 7. Banana 8. Redwood 9. Fig tree.

A Child's First Library of Learning

Flowers and Trees

Time-Life Books Inc. is a wholly owned subsidiary of
Time Incorporated.
Time-Life Books, Alexandria, Virginia
Children's Publishing

Director:	Robert H. Smith
Associate Director:	R. S. Wotkyns III
Editorial Director:	Neil Kagan
Promotion Director:	Kathleen Tresnak
Editorial Consultants:	Jacqueline A. Ball
	Andrew Gutelle

Editorial Supervision by:
International Editorial Services Inc.
Tokyo, Japan

Editor:	C. E. Berry
Editorial Research:	Miki Ishii
Design:	Kim Bolitho
Writer:	Pauline Bush
Educational Consultants:	Janette Bryden
	Laurie Hanawa
Translation:	Ronald K. Jones

TIME
LIFE ®

Library of Congress Cataloging in Publication Data
Flowers and trees.
    p.   cm. — (A Child's first library of learning)
    Summary: Presents in question and answer format information
about how all kinds of plants live, breathe, and reproduce. An
activities section is included.
    ISBN 0-8094-4857-2.   ISBN 0-8094-4858-0 (lib. bdg.)
    1. Plants—Miscellanea—Juvenile literature.
2. Flowers—Miscellanea—Juvenile literature. 3. Trees—
Miscellanea—Juvenile literature. [1. Plants—Miscellanea.
2. Questions and answers.]   I. Time-Life Books.   II. Series.
QK49.F55 1988   581—dc19   88-20155
©1988 Time-Life Books Inc.
©1983 Gakken Co. Ltd.

Fifth printing 1992. Printed in U.S.A.
Published simultaneously in Canada.

TIME-LIFE is a trademark of Time Warner Inc. U.S.A.

Time-Life Books Inc. offers a wide range of fine publications,
including home video products. For subscription information, call
1-800-621-7026, or write TIME-LIFE BOOKS, P.O. Box C-32068,
Richmond, Virginia 23261-2068.